# Where's Boaz? :

## IDK, I'm Tired of Kissing Frogs Too

## Nevada York

# Dedication

To all the women in their season of singleness, keep pressing and keep gleaning.

# Table of Contents

# 1

## Always the Brides-Maid…

“Did you hear that Tiffany and Renee are both getting married?”

“Renee?” I asked. “I had heard about Tiffany, but not Renee.”

“Yes, girl,” my friend answered. “Renee, ran into one of her guy friends from college at the grocery store like two weeks ago and now they’re getting married. She’s going to ask you to be one of her brides-maid.”

“What?” I whispered underneath my breath.

“I said that they’re getting married! She finally got her *Boaz*,” my friend emphasized and continued, “I think the date is set for June, which is in a couple of months, she doesn’t know if she wants an outdoor or indoor…maybe a beach wedding, probably not because Renee wouldn’t take a chance on the weather ruining her hair or make-up.”

I stopped listening when I heard the word “Boaz.” No, who am I kidding? I really stopped listening when she said Renee only met her soon to be husband two weeks ago. I was happy for Renee, but disheartened at the same time. When would my season come to get married? It felt like I've been waiting forever for my Boaz.

# 2

## To Glean is to Capture

So who is Boaz? Let's go back over a thousand years ago to the nation of Israel. The book of Ruth in the Bible focuses on three main people:

- Naomi: A widow who lost her husband and two sons while living in a foreign land called

  Moab

- Ruth: A Moabitess. The daughter-in-law of Naomi who is also a widow due to the death

  of Naomi's son.

- Boaz: A great man of wealth, who owned the field where Ruth gleaned for food in Israel. Too many, Boaz and Ruth represent one of the greatest love stories in the Bible.

So how did Ruth **capture** the heart of Boaz? After leaving Israel due to a famine, Naomi returned years later to her homeland along with Ruth. Boaz noticed Ruth as she was **gleaning** in his field for grain for her and Naomi. Chapter Two in the book of Ruth describes what happened next was the beginning of their love story…

- Ruth was working hard when Boaz noticed her. (She wasn't

focused on herself)

- Ruth showed Boaz respect during their first interaction. (Humbled herself when he acknowledged her)
- Boaz made it a point to inform his laborers to purposely leave extra grain on the ground for Ruth. (Displayed his desire to be her provider and protector)
- After sharing the details of the day with her mother-in-law, Ruth listened carefully to the instructions of her elder and followed Naomi's plan to further impress Boaz. (She listened)

# 3

## Gotta Have a Plan

What was this awesome plan Naomi shared with Ruth win Boaz's heart? Naomi told Ruth:

1. Where and when to make the next contact with Boaz
2. Wash herself
3. Anoint herself with perfumes
4. Get dressed for the occasion
5. Go down to the threshing floor where Boaz would be found that night
6. Do not make herself known to him until he is through eating and drinking
7. Mark the place where he shall lie down for the night
8. Go in and uncover his feet
9. Lay down at his feet
10. Listen to what Boaz tells her to do *(Dakes Annotated Bible)*

The Tenfold plan that Naomi instructed to Ruth was successful!

Can women today use Naomi's plan to be found by a "Boaz"? Absolutely! Now granted, uncovering a man's feet while he sleeps then laying down at his feet may sound a bit unconventional, but what do you have to lose? All kidding aside, when Boaz discovered Ruth laying at his feet, he immediately began the effort to become her **kinsman redeemer**. One part to pay attention to is that Ruth was obedient and moved swiftly to follow Naomi- an older wiser woman instructions. Side note, Naomi was aware of Boaz's godly character so please don't attempt to lay at any man's feet!

The next day Boaz- with a sense of urgency took the necessary steps to make Ruth his wife and the elders of the town blessed their marriage. In looking back at Ruth, she always managed to be busy laboring, had an attitude of selflessness, and more importantly, she was obedient with a heart unto the Lord. Who knows? If you're in the right place at the right time, the Lord can certainly write your love story if you allow Him to do so. Just remember to keep your gleaning gloves handy! I never leave home without them!

So what do you do while waiting on Boaz besides gleaning in the field? Well, you're bound to be disappointed by a few "fake Boaz's". Maybe, you will have to kiss a couple of frogs until you meet your true Boaz. However, there are a few things you can do while you wait-especially during those times of loneliness. You should continue to wait expectantly (Psalm 27:14). One of the best pieces of advice I received while waiting is to:

- Pray
- Study the Word
- Thank God Continuously

# *Don't Settle!*

## 4

## Ruth Reality Chart: Self-Check

Are you staying busy like Ruth? Are you being a blessing to someone like she was to Naomi? Let's take a look at the chart below to check your reality.

### Ruth Reality Chart

| Ruth's Attributes | Ruth's Reality |
|---|---|
| Obedience<br>(Submission to Another's Authority) | Respectful and Humble to Boaz<br>Listened and Followed Naomi's Instructions |
| Blessing to Someone<br>(Having a Positive Influence on Others) | Supported Her Mother-in-Law<br>Loved Her Unconditionally |
| Hard Working<br>(Stay Busy While Waiting) | Gleaned All Day Long<br>Hard Worker and Dedicated |

Ask yourself the following:

Are you being OBEDIENT? ______________________________

(All the time, sometime, none of the time)

Are you a BLESSING TO SOMEONE? ________________________

(All the time, sometime, none of the time)

Are you a DEDICATED HARD WORKER? ____________________

(All the time, sometime, none of the time)

Please elaborate and share your examples:

____________________________________________

____________________________________________

____________________________________________

____________________________________________

What are some ways that you can become MORE obedient?

____________________________________________

How can you CONTINUE to be a blessing to someone?

____________________________________________

Are there additional activities/volunteering that you can do to ILLUSTRATE your hard work?

____________________________________________

____________________________________________

____________________________________________

____________________________________________

**5**

# Trust God & His Timing

One other item to remember when faced with the setback of heartbreak…TRUST GOD, don't trust your emotions while you wait because emotions can change like the wind. As televangelist Joyce Meyer once said, *"When God withholds a desire, it's only because He wants to bestow something that He knows is better."* Those words may be hard to absorb, but you should let them penetrate your soul while you wait and continue to trust God.

Contrary to popular belief, being single doesn't mean that you walk around with a big "S" pinned on your blouse because you're ashamed of your "singleness." Embrace your singleness until Boaz comes along. As King Solomon said, *"To everything there is a season, a time for every purpose under Heaven (Ecclesiastes 3:1)."* If you find yourself struggling during your Season of Singleness follow the advice of Pastor Steven Furtick:

- Know There's a PURPOSE in Your Season
- Call "Single Season" BEAUTIFUL, God Makes Everything Beautiful in its Time

- Tis Your Season to Trust God, TRUST God's Timing
- Stay Close to GOD, So You're Near When Your Turn Comes

So where is your Boaz? When will your Season of Singleness be over? Idk, but I believe that it's important to emulate the characteristics and attributes of Ruth as she captured the heart of Boaz. Be encouraged and keep those gleaning gloves on!

# Important Vocabulary Words

**Capture**: *An act of catching, winning, or gaining control*

**Gleaning**: *To gather grain or other produce left by reapers*

**Kinsman Redeemer**: *The relative who restores or preserves the full community rights of disadvantaged family members. The concept arises from God's covenant relationship with Israel and points to the redemption of humanity in Jesus Christ*

***Don't Settle!***

***Keep holding on to the promises of God!***

## Encouraging Words of Wisdom to Memorize During Your Season of Waiting Expectantly!

**Galatians 6:9 (NIV)**

*"Let us not become weary in doing good, for at the proper time we will reap a harvest if we* ***do not give up****."*

**Psalm 27:14 (NIV)**

*"****Wait*** *for the Lord; be strong and take heart and* ***wait*** *for the Lord."*

**Jeremiah 29:11 (NIV)**

*"For I know the plans I have for you," declares the Lord, "plans to* ***prosper*** *you and not to harm you, plans to give you* ***hope*** *and a* ***future****."*

*"When God withholds a desire, it is only because He wants to bestow something that He knows is* ***better****!"* – Joyce Meyers

www.ingramcontent.com/pod-product-compliance
Lightning Source LLC
Chambersburg PA
CBHW032136050726
47590CB00008B/3127

*9780692164921*